PHILOSOPHY

of

PRESCHOOLERS

(because we all need a break from being grown-up)

Philosophy of Preschoolers
is dedicated to:

Clémentine and Anna, of course,
as well as the wonderful staff at
Arbutus Grove Preschool who honor
the magic of childhood.

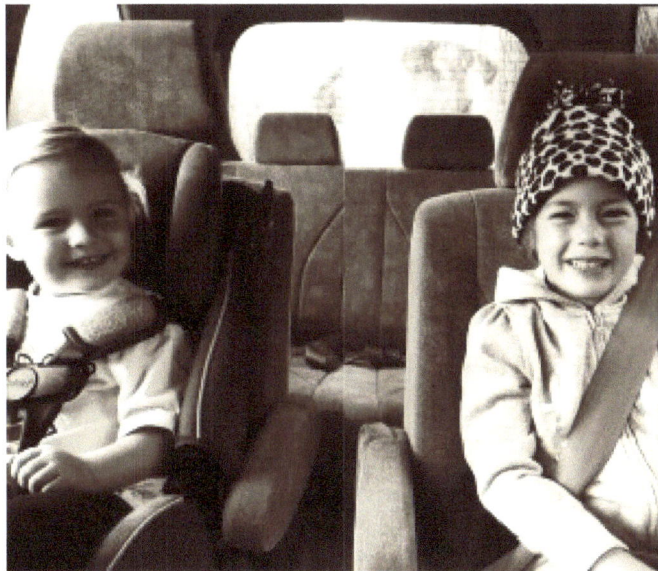

"Enjoy the little things, for one day you may look back and realize they were the big things."

- Robert Brault

Table Of Contents

Table Of Contents

Origins of
Philosophy of Preschoolers

On May 1st 2012 I was diagnosed with a rare, untreatable, and life threatening autoimmune disease of the bile ducts and liver with the tongue twisting name Primary Sclerosing Cholangitis. This was a complete shock. The disease was found during routine blood testing for life insurance. I hadn't been feeling sick. In a few nauseating seconds I went from being a healthy, globe trotting mother of three girls to being told that I had a disease that, if it didn't kill me first, would eventually mean I would require a liver transplant. Just like that, one chapter of my life slammed shut. What I didn't realize at the time was that in the same moment another chapter opened.

I started meditating, shedding anything in my life that felt inauthentic, eating copious amounts of kale, writing (which had always been my lifelong passion), and more importantly, FINISHING what I wrote. I tried to pay attention to all the "little" things that I had previously taken for granted, such as hilariously random and at times blindingly insightful conversations between my youngest daughter Clémentine (then 4) and her cousin Anna (then 3) on their way to preschool in the backseat of my mini-van.

These preschool conversations made me laugh and made me think. They gave me a break from being a grown-up for twenty precious minutes every day. They also provided insight into how, as we morph from childhood to adulthood, most of us try to cover up how bizarre, emotional, hilarious, and unique we truly are. This, I concluded, is a damn shame. Preschoolers offer us an un-shellacked lesson in humanity. I hope you enjoy it as much as I did.

Precious Talk

CLEM: "When we die, do our skeletons go up to heaven?"

ME: "No. Just our souls."

ANNA: "Clem. What colour is your house?"

CLEM: (I see in the rearview mirror she is poking her side) "Mom – this hard 'fing here, is it my soul?"

ME: "No, that would be your rib."

ANNA: "Clem! I was talking! You need to listen. What colour is your -?"

CLEM: (still poking rib) "I actually think this hard 'fing is my soul."

ANNA: "Stop interrupting me Clem! My house is white and another colour of white. Clem, what colour is-"

CLEM: (still touching rib) "I know I can feel my soul in here."

ME: "Our house is brown with blue doors Anna."

ANNA: "Clem! When I am talking you need to listen!"

CLEM: (exasperated sigh). "No, I don't need to listen. What you were saying wasn't very interesting anyway."

ANNA: "But I was talking!"

CLEM: "Talking isn't precious Anna."

Pretty Panther Hat

NB: Clementine received a fleece panther toque from her older cousin and insisted on wearing it to school the next day, despite the fact it was 23 degrees outside.

ANNA: "You have a really pretty hat Clem."

CLEM: "It's a panther hat."

ANNA: "It's really pretty."

CLEM: "And panthers have claws and they can scraaaaaaaaatch people and their blood spurts EVERYWHERE." (makes scratching, growling panther noises)

ANNA: "I like your pretty hat Clem."

Dinseyland
Home Of Dora And Flying Saucers

NB: I am not misspelling "Disneyland" – that was how they were pronouncing it and I think "Dinseyland" has a better ring anyway...

CLEM: "Mom, do you think one day we can go to Dinseyland?"

ANNA: "What's Dinseyland?"

CLEM: "Don't you know Anna? It's where Dora lives."

ANNA: "I want to go to! I want to go to Dinseyland and see Dora!"

CLEM: "Mom, is Dinseyland in the clouds?"

ME: "No, it's in California."

CLEM: "Are there flying saucers in California?"

ME: "That's an interesting question. Some people say there are and some people say there aren't."

CLEM: "I don't want to go there if there are flying saucers."

ANNA: "My mommy used to live in California."

ME: "That's right Anna, your Mom and Dad did live in California before you were born."

CLEM: "Anna, did your Mom see any flying saucers?"

ANNA: (thinking about this) "I don't know if she saw any flying saucers. Are flying saucers bad Clem?"

CLEM: "Yes, they pick people up and then BOOM them."

ANNA: "I think they crash into houses."

CLEM: "I don't like flying saucers."

ANNA: "Me neither."

Anarchy

CLEM: "There's a moose!"

ME: "I don't think that was a moose, I think it was probably a deer."

CLEM: "It was just a little tiny baby moose, he was sooooooooooooo cute, he was sooooooooooooo tiny! Did you see the baby moose Anna?"

ANNA: (waking up from her morning reverie) "YES! I see that baby moose." (Impossible, as moose miles behind us now)

ME: "I think it was a deer guys. Do you know what a baby deer is called? A baby deer like you saw Clem is called a fawn."

CLEM: "I don't like that word."

ME: "Well, that's just what baby deer are called…fawns."

CLEM: "I don't like it." (Silence in car for a few seconds)

ANNA: "I know the word fawn, but I like to just call them deer sometimes instead." (few seconds pause)

"I just call them deer sometimes."

(she is clearly really thinking about the deer/fawn issue)

CLEM: "I call them moose."

The Terrible Fate Of Coochie The Cow-Rabbit

NB. "Coochie" is the black and white spotted wild rabbit who last year lived around Clem's preschool and was named "Coochie" by the kids.

CLEM:	(sad voice) "Nobody has seen Coochie this year."
ANNA:	"Coochie! That's a silly word Clem."
CLEM:	"Coochie is our school rabbit. He is a cow rabbit."
ANNA:	"A cow rabbit! You're silly Clem."
CLEM:	"No I'm not! He looks just like a cow except he doesn't have horns but he has bunny ears."
ME:	"It's true. He does look like a cow, except smaller and with no horns."
CLEM:	(sad voice): "Except he's gone. I think today I'm going to draw a picture of coochie. Where do you think he is?"
ME:	(thinking of cougar spotted roaming around in woods behind the preschool last year) "Well, maybe he's still on summer vacation! Do you remember how you went to France this summer-"
ANNA:	"Yes!" (Anna didn't actually go to France this summer)
ME:	"Well, maybe Coochie is still on vacation in France! Maybe he's having so much fun that he doesn't want to come back yet!" (much thinking in the back seat)
CLEM:	"Or maybe he just died."
ANNA:	"Yeah. I think he just died."

Coochie And The Magical Poo

ANNA: "Clem – you know what? Yesterday morning at school we found deer poo by the swing!"

CLEM: "That's not true."

ANNA: "It is true. Eleni touched the poo and then my teacher picked it up and put it in the garbage can. My teacher touched the poo!" (much mirth from Anna)

CLEM: "Actually Anna, I don't think it was deer poo."

ANNA: "It was deer poo. My teacher said it was deer poo when Eleni touched it."

CLEM: (whispers) "Actually Anna, I think it was a magical poo."

ANNA: "A magical poo? What's that – a magical poo?"

CLEM: "I think it was Coochie who came during the night and did a poo. It was like…magical! That means Coochie has come back to us!" (hugs self in glee)

ANNA: "Yay!" (Anna and Clem join together in a rousing cheer)

Lesson In Self-Acceptance

On picking up Anna in the afternoon, her teacher bequeathes me a plastic bag full of her wet clothes, explaining that she had two little accidents at school. Anna is very quiet and thoughtful as we start the drive home.

ANNA: "I do pee in my pants at school sometimes."

ME: "Everyone does that. It's totally okay Anna."

CLEM: "I used to pee in my pants at school when I was in the 3/4s, but I don't now that I'm in the 4/5s, right Mom?"

ME: "Yup. But it's okay for anyone to have a pee accident. It happens."

ANNA: "Yeah. It's okay to have an accident."

ME: "It certainly is okay."

ANNA: "Can you tell my Mom that it's okay to pee in your pants at school?"

ME: "She already knows that. Everyone knows it's okay."

ANNA: "Yeah. It's okay."

ME: "Sure it is."

ANNA: "It's really okay."

ME: "Of course it is. Everyone had pee accidents sometimes."

CLEM: "So that means you pee in your pants sometimes too Mom?"

God Hangs Ten

CLEM: "Mom, do you know when I'm going to die?"

ME: "No I don't. Nobody knows for sure when they're going to die."

CLEM: "Does God know when we're going to die?"

ME: "…I guess maybe God might know."

CLEM: (big sigh) "I sure wish God would come to shore and tell us."

ME: "Come to shore?"

CLEM: "Yeah. I wish he would come to shore and tell us when we're going to die."

ME: "Where is God coming to shore from? Is he in the ocean?"

CLEM: "He's lives on a surfboard mom, didn't you know that?"

ME: "Actually I did NOT know that."

CLEM: "That's the way it is. God lives on a surfboard in the milky wave."

Scary Spiders With Top-Bottoms

ANNA: "My mom doesn't like spiders."

ME: "I know that. She's always been a bit scared of them." (make that terrified)

ANNA: "She doesn't like big ones that jump at her."

ME: "I don't mind spiders, but I don't think I would really like them jumping at me either."

ANNA: "When we were at the house on the lake my mom saw a spider that made her scream."

ME: "Really?"

ANNA: "Yes. It had a top-bottom."

ME: "A top-bottom?"

ANNA: "Yes. It was very fat and had a top-bottom. It was a top-bottom spider. It was very scary."

ME: "I'll bet."

ANNA: "Even though I was scared I looked at it."

ME: "You`re very brave."

ANNA: "Yes, people who look at top-bottom spiders are very brave."

Full Of Brains

CLEM: "This is how it works Anna – our heart is full of blood and then the blood goes through our
          brains and then into our hands."

ME: (perplexed) "How does the blood go from your brains to your hands?"

CLEM: "I have brains in my hand Mom."

ANNA: "Where? Show me!" (Clem shows Anna the veins on the inside of her wrist)

CLEM: "See these blue 'fings here Anna? These are my brains."

ANNA: (concerned) "Do they hurt Clem?"

CLEM: "No, I have brains all through my body. They make me strong."

ANNA: "Do I have brains in my hands?" (Anna holds out her arm to Clem for inspection and Clem
          points at veins in Anna's wrist)

CLEM: "Yes! Look at all your brains! Right there!"

ANNA: (shrieking with excitement) "Look at all my brains Auntie Laura! I have brains all over my
          arm!"

ME: "Amazing."

Further Thoughts On Souls

CLEM: "Mom, when we die does our skin go to Heaven?"

ME: "No."

CLEM: "What about our blood and bones and stuff?"

ME: "All that stays on earth. It's just our souls that go up to heaven."

CLEM: "Where IS my soul?"

ME: "Souls aren't really solid things. They're like…ummmm…your thoughts and your feelings and -."

CLEM: "Why can't I see my soul?"

ME: (trying to think of a good answer while not having a head-on collision) "Well…it's kinda like love. You know when you hug someone you love it feels all warm and nice?"

CLEM: "Yes."

ME: "Even though you can't see or touch love, you know it's there, right?"

CLEM: (nods) "Yeah!" (Drive on a little farther, then I notice in the rear view mirror that Clem keeps blowing on the palm of her hand)

ME: "Did you hurt your hand?"

CLEM: "No. I can feel the air when I blow on my hand, but I can't see it. Is that what my soul is like?"

ME: "That's EXACTLY what it's like."

Anna's Thumb-Sucking Haiku

CLEM: "Anna's sucking her thumb again Mom."

ME: "I see that."

CLEM: "When Anna sucks her thumb it means she's tired."

ME: "Does it?"

CLEM: "Yup. When Anna is tired she sucks her thumb. That's just the way it is."

ME: "I think you're right Clem."

ANNA: (pops thumb out of mouth) "It's not just because I'm tired. There are lots of reasons."

CLEM: "Like what?"

ANNA: (reinserts thumb and gazes up at sky). "I suck my thumb when there is blue sky. The car is driving on the road. Clouds."

The Girl Who Threw Witches

CLEM: "Asha in your class was really naughty at school."

ANNA: "Asha cries a lot. It's really annoying."

CLEM: "She was naughty today during outside time. She was throwing witches at the teachers."

ANNA: "I was on the monkey bars when she was throwing the witches. The teachers told her 'no!'. Then she cried."

ME: (confused) "Where did Asha find witches to throw?"

CLEM: "They're just like…you know…all over the ground. There's witches everywhere at the play ground."

ANNA: "It's naughty to throw witches at teachers."

CLEM: "Yes. The teachers always say 'the witches belong on the ground!'"

ME: "Witches?"

CLEM: "Yes. Witches."

ME: "Ohhhhhhh! Don't you mean 'wood chips'?"

CLEM: "No mom. Witches."

The Upside Of Adoption

CLEM: "Why does Kate have brown skin and her sister have white skin?"

ANNA: "Sissy in my class has brown skin. It's nice."

ME: "Kate has browner skin than her sister because she was adopted from China."

CLEM: "What does 'adopted' mean?"

ME: "Um. It means Kate didn't grow in her Mommy's tummy. Her mommy went to find her in China." (lame explanation, but it's only 8:00am)

CLEM: "Was I adopted?"

ME: "No. You grew in my tummy."

ANNA: "Was I adopted?"

ME: "No, you grew in your mommy's tummy." (much thinking going on in back seat)

CLEM: "I think Jean-Marc was adopted because he has brown skin."

ME: "No. I know his parents and he's not adopted."

CLEM: "I'm not so sure about that."

ME: "I'm pretty sure Clem."

CLEM: (big sigh) "It's just not fair. I want to be adopted."

ANNA: (bigger sigh) "Me too. It's not fair."

ME: "I'm sure being adopted is great, but why do you guys want to be adopted?"

CLEM: "If I was adopted then I would have brown skin like Kate and Jean-Marc and Sissi."

ME: "That's not really the way it wor-"

ANNA: "I want brown skin too."

CLEM: "White skin is so ANNOYING."

ANNA: "You know Auntie Laura, it's really hard to have white skin. It's just too boring."

A Logical Explanation For Body Hair

This weekend we cheered on all the marathoners running up and down our street (way to go you guys!). A very hairy specimen wearing a teeny, tiny tank top ran by and Clem stopped in the middle of the sidewalk and watched his receding back, riveted.

CLEM: "That sure is some furry skin!"

ME: (once I'd stopped laughing) "Why do you think the man has furry skin like that?" (Clem thinks for a while)

CLEM: "I'm pretty sure that he must have eaten a bear."

ME: "Oh?"

CLEM: "Yes. Now all that bear fur is growing through his skin."

The Underwear Makes The Person

CLEM: "Mom?"

ME: "Yes Clem?"

CLEM: "Do you know that the people Kate draws at school aren't real?"

ME: "Why aren't they real?"

CLEM: "She just draws a circle for the head and then a big circle for the body and then sticks for the arms and legs."

ME: "That sounds like a pretty good person."

CLEM: "No. Her people don't even have any clothes."

ME: "Maybe her people are naked."

CLEM: "No. Actually, her people don't even have underwear or bums."

ME: "Oh."

CLEM: "I told Kate her people couldn't be real if they didn't have underwear or bums. My people ALWAYS have underwear and bums."

ME: "Do they really?"

CLEM: "Yes. Underwear and bums are what make people real."

The Girls Who Doesn't Like Pink

CLEM: "There is a girl in my class named Leily."

ME: "What's she like?"

CLEM: "She doesn't like pink or princesses or anything that girls like."

ME: "She doesn't even like pink?"

CLEM: "No. Her favorite colour is black."

ME: "Wow."

CLEM: "Do you think she can still be a girl if she doesn't like pink and princesses and girl 'fings?"

ME: "Girls can like anything they want, you know."

CLEM: "Oh." (thinks for a while) "I guess then she's just made differently than me."

Hidden Benefits Of Pee Accidents

ANNA: "I did two pee accidents at school today, but that's okay."

ME: "Of course it's okay."

ANNA: "Yeah. It's okay."

ME: "Definitely."

CLEM: "Doing pee accidents at school is SO much fun."

ME: "Fun? Why is it fun?"

CLEM: "Because when you do a pee at school you get to put on a new outfit."

ANNA: "I like new outfits."

CLEM: "You never know what clothes are going to be in your bag. It's such a fun surprise."

ANNA: "Peeing at school is so much fun."

CLEM: "I want to pee at school and put new clothes on EVERY day!"

ANNA: "Me too!"

Nervous Hairs

Clem, who usually goes to school blissfully content with the fact that with her hair looks like she's stuck her finger in a light socket, spends half an hour in the morning brushing her hair in front of the mirror. As I am zipping up her sweatshirt she pats it down again.

CLEM: "My hairs are really nervous this morning."

ME: "Are they? Why? You did a good job brushing them. They look beautiful."

CLEM: "Are you sure they look great?"

ME: "I'm sure."

CLEM: "They don't look like (shakes head) all crazy and blablabla?"

ME: "No. They don't look all crazy and blablabla. They look lovely." (Clem kisses me)

CLEM: "Ok Mom. I'll tell them not to be so nervous."

The Confetti Dust Continuum

Clem sneezes in the van on the way to school.

ANNA: "Bless you Clem."

ME: "Are you getting a cold Clem?"

CLEM: "No, I'm not getting a cold. I'm sneezing because of all of this confetti in your car." (Clem glances around van with disdain)

ME: "Confetti? I don't see any confetti in my car."

ANNA: "What is confetti Auntie Laura?"

CLEM: "I meant DUST Anna. There's too much dust in your car Mom. It's really dirty."

ME: "Ah well…yes, I guess that's true."

ANNA: "Where is the confetti?"

CLEM: "Dust is inside the car Anna. Confetti is what's outside the car in the air."

ANNA: (looking out window) "I want to see the confetti!"

CLEM: "It's invisible, but it's there. Dust makes me sneeze inside and confetti makes me sneeze outside."

ANNA: "Me too."

Tastes Like Roast Chicken

CLEM: "Anna, does your Mommy shave her legs? "

ANNA: "What did you say Clem?"

CLEM: "Does your Mommy shave the hair on her legs?"

ANNA: "What hair?"

CLEM: (shows Anna her forearm) "You see, hair like this on your body."

ANNA: "I don't know."

CLEM: (takes a bite of her forearm) "I eat my hair."

ME: "You do!? That's gross Clem."

CLEM: "No, actually it's really good."

ANNA: "What does your hair taste like Clem? Does it taste like candy?"

CLEM: "It tastes like roast chicken."

Marriage

CLEM: "It's so funny. Jean-Marc doesn't even realize I have a crush on him."

ME: "You have a crush on Jean-Marc? What does that mean?"

CLEM: "It means I want to marry him."

ME: "Really?"

CLEM: "I'm sad though because he wants to marry Grace."

ME: "On no!"

CLEM: "Baxter wants to marry Grace too."

ME: *sigh* "You'll find going through life that often all the guys like the same girls."

CLEM: "I told Baxter and Jean-Marc that I wanted to marry Grace too but Baxter said I couldn't because she's a girl. Can a girl marry a girl?"

ME: "Sure. In our country a girl can marry a girl."

CLEM: "Can a boy marry a boy?"

ME: "Yup. In Canada a boy can marry a boy too."

CLEM: "Can a boy marry a girl?"

ME: "In our country pretty much anyone who is in love and wants to get married can go ahead and get married."

CLEM: (thinks about this for a while). "That seems fair."

Kid Nappers

CLEM: "Mom, what's a kidnapper?"

ME: "It's a very bad person."

CLEM: "Is it a bad guy like a robber or a witch?"

ME: "I guess it could be."

CLEM: "Do kidnappers give kids poison or something that makes them have naps even when they don't want to?"

ME: (trying to figure this out until light dawns) "Oh! Did you think kidnappers make kids have naps?"

CLEM: "Yes. That's why they're called 'Kid Nappers'."

ME: "Actually kidnappers don't have anything to do with naps."

CLEM: "Whew! That's a relief. I hate naps."

The Cosmic Law of Zippers

CLEM: "You know what Mom?"

ME: "What Clem?"

CLEM: "I'm such a big girl now. Yesterday I did up my zipper by myself. It's because I'm five."

ME: "Wow."

ANNA: "I can't do up my own zipper yet."

CLEM: "That's because you're only three Anna. You won't be able to do zip up your zipper until you're five."

ANNA: (sotto voce) "I think that I'll be able to do my zipper when I'm four."

CLEM: "No! In life, Anna, kids can't do up their zippers until they're five."

ANNA: "Four."

CLEM: (big sigh) "In this world, Anna, little kids can't do up their own zippers until they're five."

ANNA: "That's not fair."

CLEM: "In this world and this life Anna, that's just the rule about zippers."

Mindful Eating

CLEM: "Yesterday at school Anna and I got to eat lunch together at the same table."

ME: "Wow! That sounds like fun. Was it fun?"

ANNA: "Yes."

ME: "What was your favorite thing about it?"

CLEM: "You know…talking and laughing and stuff. Also, Anna looked so cute in her little dress. I like having lunch with her when she looks so cute."

ME: "What about you Anna? What was your favorite part?"

ANNA: (thinks for a while) "My lunch."

Girls Who Scream

Clem was telling me about how Anna and another member of the 3 year olds class got to have lunch in the 4 /5 classroom with Clem.

ME: "So you got to have lunch with Anna?"

CLEM: "Yup."

ME: "That must have been a special treat."

CLEM: "It was SO fun. We got to sit at the same table"

ME: "Were there any other 3 year olds from Anna's class who had lunch with you?"

CLEM: (dark look) "Yes. Cecile."

ME: "Did you have a nice chat with Cecile too?"

CLEM: "No."

ME: "Why not?"

CLEM: "You know Mom. She's one of those girls."

ME: "Uh…no, I don't know."

CLEM: "She's one of those girls who screams."

ME: "Oh."

CLEM: "Screaming girls are very rude."

ME: "Did you at least get to talk with her a little bit?"

CLEM: "No. It is impossible to talk with girls who scream."

The Lonliest Place

Anna and Clem are playing upstairs in her bedroom after school.

ANNA: "Don't take my dolly Clem, I just have to go to the bathroom."

CLEM: "Do you want me to come with you?"

ANNA: "Why?"

CLEM: "Sitting on the toilet all by yourself can be really lonely."

ANNA: "Oh."

CLEM: "And scary."

ANNA: "OK. Let's go!"

CLEM: "Just wait a second Anna. I need to do something first."

ANNA: "What do you need to do Clem?"

CLEM: "I need to bring some stuffies to keep us company too."

Does Celine Dion Fart?

Somehow the discussion in the back of the van turns to farts...

CLEM: "I don't fart. In fact, I've never farted in my life Anna. Not even once."

ME: "Everybody farts Clem. Even you."

ANNA: "My baby sister farts a lot."

ME: "Babies do that. It's pretty funny."

ANNA: "You know who else farts a lot?"

ME: "Who?"

ANNA: "My Dad."

ME: "Oh."

CLEM: "I've never farted because I'm a princess and princesses don't fart."

ME: "Everybody farts Clem. Even princesses."

ANNA: "Yeah Clem. Everybody farts." We all reflect on this profound truth.

ANNA: "I don't think Celine Dion farts." (nb. Anna and her father love Celine Dion and watch her music videos on a daily basis)

CLEM: "Is she a princess?"

ANNA: "A bit...I'm not sure...maybe she's a princess. The thing is...the thing is that her dresses are too fancy for farting."

CLEM: "She must be a princess then."

Silly

After Clem's day with the stomach flu she has a barf-free night and is sitting in front of her morning bagel and honey.

Me: "How are you feeling this morning sweetie?" (Clem Purses her lips and thinks about this for a while.)

Clem: "Actually, I'm feeling really silly."

Eerily Like Playdough

Cleaning Clem up after she barfed five times in Jayne's car on the way home from preschool."

Me: "Did you feel sick all day sweetie?"

Clem: "Yes. I even threw up at school."

Me: "You did? Did you make it to the bathroom?"

Clem: "No. I threw up on the diamond shape on the carpet in the art room during morning story time."

Me: "Why didn't they call me to come and pick you up?"

Clem: "They didn't realize I threw up."

Me: "Didn't they notice the barf on the carpet?"

Clem: "They did but they just thought it was playdough."

Me: "Did they clean it up?"

Clem: "Mom, they don't clean up playdough on the carpet until the end of the day."

Just Plain Bums

Clem and Anna are very into the "Pretty Ponies" TV show at the moment.

CLEM: "Anna? What's your cutie mark?"

ANNA: "What do you mean Clem?"

CLEM: "You know how all the Pretty Ponies have cutie marks on their bums? Like Rainbow Dash has a rainbow and Applejack has apples and Fluttershy has butterflies-"

ANNA: "Oh yeah. I forgot about that."

CLEM: "What's yours?"

ANNA: "I don't know. Maybe a spoon. What's yours Clem?"

CLEM: "Mine is a heart made of bows."

ANNA: "Can I see it?"

CLEM: "No. Even I can't see it because it's behind me. But it's there. It's true I have a cutie mark on my bum, right Mom?"

ME: "Actually no Clem. Not yet anyway. You can get one when you're a little bit older. It's called a tattoo."

ANNA: "You mean we don't have cutie marks on our bums right now?"

ME: "No. I don't have one either."

CLEM: "I want a cutie mark! That's not fair."

ME: "We don't have them because we're not Pretty Ponies. We're people."

ANNA: "That's not very fair."

CLEM: "You mean people have just plain bums?"

ME: "That's right. Just plain bums."

CLEM: "I hate being a person with just a plain bum."

ANNA: "Me too! I hate plain bums."

Won-Tons in Bed

Clem is climbing up into Franck's and my massive king sized bed.

CLEM: "I like Daddy's side of the bed better."

ME: "Why?"

CLEM: "Your side smells like a tornado."

ME: "A what?"

CLEM.   "A tornado. Well…it's not exactly a tornado smell. More like chinese food. That's it! Your side smells just like chinese food."

Stop Destructing Me

CLEM: "Anna, do you know Rainbow Dash in the Pretty Ponies?"

ANNA: "I had french toast for breakfast this morning."

CLEM: "Rainbow Dash flies SO fast. She's the fastest -."

ANNA: "I had LOTS of maple syrup on my french toast."

CLEM: "I can run as fast as Rainbow-"

ANNA: "I love maple syrup. It's so delicious."

CLEM: "I don't want to hear about maple syrup! Stop destructing me Anna!"

My Name For Today

ME: "Good morning Clemmie."

CLEM: "Don't call me Clemmie."

ME: "Why not?"

CLEM: "Today my name is Princess Celestia."

"The Mean, Ugly Witch
(Otherwise Known as Mom)

Flu. 2:00am. Clem's fever hovering around 104 C. Trying to get her to take two Advil.

ME: "Come on sweetie. I know they don't taste good but they'll make you feel better."

CLEM: "Noooooooooooo. I hate them."

ME: "I want you to take them because I love you and I want your fever to go down."

CLEM: "You're just making me take them because you're mean!"

ME: "No. The Advil will make you feel better."

CLEM: "You're making me take them because you're a mean witch."

ME: "I'm not a mean witch. I'm your Mom."

CLEM: "You're an ugly, mean witch and you're trying to feed me poison."

ME: "I'm not, actually."

CLEM: "Yes you are. I think you even have a wart on your nose."

Forgetting

CLEM: "Sometimes I get so busy I forget."

ME: "What do you mean?"

CLEM: "Sometimes I get so busy at school swinging and painting and gluing and stuff that I forget the really important things."

ME: "What important things?"

CLEM: "Like the day I was born…stuff like that."

Living in The Present

ME: "What are you guys looking forward to at school today?"

CLEM: "Pretending I'm a Pretty Pony with my friends. My Pretty Pony name is Rainbow Dash."

ME: "What about you Anna?"

ANNA: "I don't know."

ME: "You don't? What fun things will you do at school tdoay?"

ANNA: "How can I know that? They haven't happened yet."

Marriage Redux

CLEM: "I think I want to marry Daddy. He's the only nice boy I know."

ME: "You can't. He's already taken."

CLEM: "I don't want to marry Grace or Jean-Marc or Baxter anymore."

ME: "Why not?"

CLEM: "They're all annoying."

ME: "Then it's probably a good idea not to marry them."

CLEM: "Who should I marry then?"

MF: "You're five. You don't have to marry anyone for a long, long time."

CLEM: "I know! I'll marry myself!"

ME: "There's a plan."

CLEM: "Yes. It will be way less annoying that way."

Sarah Sparkles

Driving out of the preschool parking lot.

ME: "Look Clem! That little girl has the same jacket as you." Clem looks out the van window

CLEM: "Oh yes. That girl's name is Sarah Sparkles."

ME: "Really?"

CLEM: "Yes, her name is Sarah Sparkles. She is so lucky because she has the coolest name in the world."

ME: "Is that her real name or just a make-up name?"

CLEM: "I guess it's sort of a make-up name."

ME: "What's her real name?"

CLEM: "Fiona."

Belly-Buttons & Little Boys

CLEM: "Christian in my class is a very random person."

ME: "Do you know what 'random' means?"

CLEM: "Hmmmmm…I'm not exactly sure but I can give you an exmaple."

ME: "OK. Shoot."

CLEM: "Like you could ask 'Do kids all have belly buttons?" and I would answer "A bowl of pasquetti!" I think that would be random."

ME: "That would be random."

CLEM: "What are belly buttons for?"

ME: "What do you think belly buttons are for?"
          Clem puts her hand over hers while she takes in a few deep breaths.

CLEM: "I think that's how we breathe…also, maybe they're just because peoples' tummies would look weird without belly buttons."

ME: "That could be."

CLEM: "When I think about it I realize that everything about belly buttons is awkward and random."

ME: "Really?"

CLEM: "Yeah. Kind of like Christian."

Eternal Allure of The Bad Boy

ANNA: "Thomas is the naughtiest boy in our class."

CLEM: "Does he get in trouble a lot?"

ANNA: "He gets Quiet Thinking Time almost every day."

CLEM: "I don't like naughty boys."

ANNA: "I like Thomas. He gives me a hug every morning. I like it when he gives me a hug."

CLEM: "But he's so naughty Anna!"

ANNA: "He is, but I still like him."

Tales of Addiction

CLEM: "Do you eat your boogers Anna?"

ANNA: "No."

CLEM: "I eat my boogers." (Anna reflects on this tidbit of information for a while)

ANNA: "In my family we eat toast and bread."

CLEM: "Actually Anna, toast is just bread that's been put in the toaster and toasted. It's the same thing."

ANNA: "I know that Clem."

CLEM: (sighs) "I'm REALLY trying to stop eating my boogers."

ANNA: "I eat toast every day."

CLEM: (sounding world-weary) "You know Anna, it's REALLY hard to stop eating boogers. They're SOOOOOOOO good." (both indulge in a moment of reflection)

ANNA: "Toast with jam is good too."

Weedwackers

We see somebody using a weedwacker on the way to preschool

Anna: "When I grow up, I'm going to buy a weedwacker."

Clem: "Me too. Weedwackers are so cool."

Anna: "But you can't get to close to them because they'll grab you. They're very dangerous."

Clem: "Do you know why they're called weedwhackers?"

Anna: "No."

Clem: "Because a weed is like grass. It's sort of the same thing."

Anna.   "Oh. That's interesting Clem."

Clem: "Wouldn't it be so funny if we had weekwhackers and we weekwhacked all the grass and flowers and everything until all there was was dirt?"

Anna: (laughing hysterically). "That would be SO funny Clem. We have to do that when we get our weekwhackers."

Clem: "Yes. It will be a great joke."

Fairy Powers

Clem: "Is there soft white bread for my lunch tomorrow?"

Me: "No. I didn't have time to get any."

Clem: "Hmph."

Me: "You say you're a magic fairy. Why can't you use your fairy powers to bake us some bread?"

Clem: "Mom! Baking is not one of my magical fairy powers. My magical fairy powers are way better than baking."

Me: "Oh, that's too bad. I'd love to have magical baking fairy powers. What are your fairy powers then?"

Clem: "Shooting lava and death rays at evil creatures."

Me: "You're right. That is better."

Earth & Sun

Anna: "Clem did you know the sun is bigger than the earth?"

Clem: "No. The earth is bigger than the sun."

Anna: "No it's not Clem the sun is HUGE."

Clem: "Mom. The earth is bigger than the sun, right?"

Me: "No. Actually Anna is right, the sun is much bigger than the earth."

Clem: "Oh. I knew that. I was just joking."

Anna: "The sun is a big ball of fire."

Clem: "Yeah. It's made up of lava and fire and evil rays and all kinds of the most dangerous things. That's what makes it so awesome."

Living Cupcakes

Clem: (Eating a cupcake) "Mom, do you know cupcakes are alive?"

Me: "Really?"

Clem: "Yes. They have little faces and little smiles. It's just that most people can't see them. I can."

Me: "So what is the cupcake doing right now?"

Clem: "He's winking at me." (proceeds to tear cupcake in half and stuff half in her mouth).

Me: "Woah! Don't you feel bad eating it if it's alive?"

Clem: "No, it's also delicious."

The Lonely Child

Anna: "Clem, do you like Christopher?"

Clem: "He's a very complicated boy so I'm not sure."

Anna: "Why is he complicated Clem?"

Clem: "I think it's because he's a lonely child."

Anna: "Why is he lonely?"

Clem: "He doesn't have any brothers and sisters so that's what we call a 'lonely child'."

Anna: "So are lonely children complicated?"

Clem: "Always."

Handy-Downs

Clem: "Big Anna gave me some handy-downs."

Anna: "What are handy-downs Clem?"

Clem: "They are clothes she doesn't use anymore so she gives them to me. That's really handy because I don't have to buy new clothes. That's why we call it handy-downs."

Anna: "That makes sense."

Black and White World

Clem: "Mom, when you were little was the world black and white?"

Me: "No. Why?"

Clem: "Well, you know how all the photos of the old-fashioned days are black and white?"

Me: "Yeah."

Clem: "Did you live in those days when everything was black and white."

Me: "Um. The world wasn't black and white then Clem. It was just the photos that were black and white. The world has always been colour."

Charlotte (14 year old daughter): "It WAS?"

Me: "Charlotte. You're not seriously telling me that you thought just because old photos are black and white that the world was black and white?"

Charlotte: "Well...yeah. That's what I thought."

Me: "Are you serious?"

Charlotte: (laughs). "Yes."

Me: "So what did you think happened? That the world was black and white and then suddenly just burst into colour?"

Clem: "Yes!"

Charlotte: "Well...yes."

Me: (laughing too hard to answer)

Fascinating

Clem: "I couldn't believe Christopher when the baby came to school for a visit."

Anna: "He was so nice to the baby."

Clem: "He was so gentle with the baby and usually all Christopher does is hit other kids. I was so surprised."

Me: "Wow."

Clem: "Yes, I realized today that Christopher is a complex boy."

Anna: "What does complex mean Clem?"

Clem: "Fascinating."

Please and Thank-Yous

I am always nagging Clémentine to remember her manners so I can't be remiss in this department.

Thank you to Clémentine and Anna and their friends for being such inimitable little souls. Thanks to Charlotte and Camille for being such wonderful big sisters and to Franck for being an amazing father to our bevy. I feel so lucky to have the Beaudrys - Jayne, Mark, Anna, & Clara - living so close and being a wonderful part of our lives.

Arbutus Grove Preschool is an unbelievably special place where they believe children should be given the time, space, and materials to learn through imagination and play. Some royalties from this book will be donated to Arbutus Grove Preschool for their many needs from swing sets to finger paint to glitter glue.

On bad days when I struggle with the health issues and mental challenges of living with PSC I remind myself that there are countless children who are fighting against the same disease with astounding grace and courage. Ten per cent of the royalties from this book will be donated to PSC Partners Seeking a Cure and earmarked for research in their honor.

As for the "please" portion, could I request that everyone sign up to be an organ donor and campaign for opt-out systems in their country? Too many lives are being lost every day due to inertia. Also, if anyone you know suffers from PSC could you please nag them to sign up for the PSC registry which is one of the best tools for finding a treatment or better yet a cure? Here is the link: https://pscpartners.patientcrossroads.org/

Finally, thank you to all the people who have told me how much they enjoy the "Philosophy of Preschoolers" posts. They are the reason this book exists.

www.ingramcontent.com/pod-product-compliance
Lightning Source LLC
LaVergne TN
LVHW072052070426
835508LV00002B/58